SERMON OUTLINES

on

Family and Home

T0317171

compiled by
Al Bryant

kregel
PUBLICATIONS

Grand Rapids, MI 49501

Sermon Outlines on Family and Home by Al Bryant

Library of Congress Cataloging-in-Publication Data
Bryant, Al (1926–
    Sermon outlines on family and home / [compiled by] Al Bryant.
        p. cm.
    1. Home—Biblical teaching—Sermons—Outlines, syllabi, etc. 2. Family—Biblical teaching—Sermons—Outlines, syllabi, etc. I. Bryant, Al, 1926–
BS680.H6S47   1996   251'.02—dc20   96-10310
                                                                CIP
ISBN 0-8254-2080-6

            2 3 4 5 6 / 07 06 05 04 03

CONTENTS

Foundations for Families

Points for Parents

Children and Their Parents

PREFACE

What is happening to the family in today's ever-accelerating world? The family, in a word, is falling apart as we enter the twenty-first century. Family relationships are breaking down, and if some of our "progressive" politicians and social experts have their way, the normal and traditional family, as instituted in Scripture and rather common in the first decades of the twentieth century, may well disappear as we enter the early decades of the twenty-first. It is my hope, as the compiler of these sermon outlines on the family and home, that this volume will stimulate new thoughts and remind all of us of the solid foundation that the Scriptures afford for family living at its best.

AL BRYANT

SCRIPTURE INDEX

A MOTHER IN ISRAEL

1 Samuel 1:27–28

The Old Testament is filled with examples of motherhood—good and bad. Samuel's mother, Hannah, is a good model for motherhood.

I. Hannah Looked upon Motherhood As a Privilege.

A. In her day, woman's one vocation was the home and motherhood.

B. Today, in many instances, women are satisfied without children.

C. A modern woman who turns her heart from the cry of motherhood deliberately turns from her sublimest throne.

D. The ones to whom the world today is the most indebted are the ones who have borne children. Martin Luther's mother was not a religious leader, but we know that she rocked the Reformation in her cradle.

II. Hannah Was a Praying Mother—"for this child I pray."

A. God pity the child who comes into a home where no one prays.

B. The heavy responsibilities of parenthood should lead us to pray.

C. If we have nothing of spiritual food to give to a child, then that child is to be pitied.

III. Hannah Recognized Her Child As God's Child.

A. She believed that he had been given to her from God.

B. She in turn "lent" him to the Lord.

C. Hannah thought there was nothing in life higher or nobler for her boy.

D. The time to start the child in the right road is in the earliest days of his life.

IV. Hannah Succeeded.

A. Hannah made good at the highest of vocations—motherhood.

B. The whole nation of Israel knew that a prophet had been born.

C. Samuel was not born a saint—he was made one by home training.

D. What we teach children concerning God makes the difference.

    1. For instance, Lot did not put God first and as a result lost his influence over his children and saw them go to damnation.

    2. Abraham, on the other hand, put God first and generations have risen up to call him blessed.

adapted from *Clovis G. Chappell*

MATERNAL PIETY

For this child I prayed: and the Lord hath given me my petition which I asked of Him (1 Sam. 1:27–28).

This text is the declaration of Hannah's conduct and experience, and the noble resolve she makes on account thereof. She refers to,

I. Her Devotional Solicitude.
A. Her condition was one of motherly sorrow and vexation.
B. Her recourse was to God by prayer.
C. She sought of the Lord a special favor.
D. For this special favor she evidently prayed most confidently.

II. The Divine Favor She Experienced.
A. God heard her supplication.
B. God was favorable to her plea.
C. God granted her the desire of her heart.

III. The Spirit Hannah Manifested.
A. Profound reverence for God. She gave Him all the glory.
B. A personal testimony as to the value of prayer.
C. An unselfish recognition of God's claim to her child.
D. A full consecration of Samuel to God's service. Herein she exhibited the power of personal religion. A noteworthy example of maternal self-denial, and a supreme concern for God's glory and her child's highest happiness. Her prayers and tears and self-denial gave to Israel one of her holiest men and most faithful prophets.

Jabez Burns

THE FOOLISH MOTHER

Genesis 27:46

Rebekah is one of the few foolish mothers mentioned in the Bible. For some reason, best known to herself, she did what no parent should ever do—developed a partiality for one of her sons and let it so far pervade her judgment as to deceive her husband.

I. Foolish is the mother who forgets to honor God when He lays a child within her arms.

II. Foolish is the mother who forgets that children are sent to her to be trained for the service of God.

III. Foolish is the mother who grieves sinfully over the loss of a child.
A. Grief can be sinful—when it fights against the will of
God.
B. Worry is also sinful and part of grieving.

IV. Foolish is the mother who is too busy with meetings and parties (in or out of the church) to live with her children.

V. Foolish is the mother who lets her daughter learn from other girls the wonderful story of life.

VI. Foolish is the mother who does not avail herself of every possible opportunity to be the best possible mother to her child.

VII. Foolish is the mother who tries to rear her children without discipline.

VIII. Foolish is the mother who encourages her son or daughter in social practices of dangerous tendencies.

IX. Foolish is the mother who loses heart and fears that the rising generation is sinking.

Joseph B. Baker

WOMEN WHO HELP

The women whose hearts stirred them up (Ex. 35:26).

Almost 200 years ago the King of Prussia, Frederick William III, found himself in great trouble. He was carrying on expensive wars, and had not money enough to accomplish his plans. But he knew that his people loved and trusted him, and he believed that they would be glad to help him. He therefore asked the women of Prussia, as many of them as wanted to help their king, to bring their jewelry of gold and silver to be melted down into money for the use of their country.

Many women brought all the jewelry they had, and for each ornament of gold or silver they received in exchange an ornament of bronze, or iron, precisely like the gold or silver ones, as a token of the king's gratitude. These iron and bronze ornaments all bore the inscription, "I gave gold for iron, 1813." These ornaments therefore became more highly prized than the gold or silver ones had been, for it was a proof that the woman had given up something for her king.

It became very unfashionable to wear any jewelry, for any other would have been a token that the wearer was not loyal to her king and country. So the Order of the Iron Cross grew up, whose members wear no ornaments except a cross of iron on the breast, and give all their surplus money to the service of their fellowmen. How gloriously prosperous some of our missionary societies would become if our people would only give their surplus jewelry and surplus money toward this God-honoring work of the world's redemption!

   I. **Praising Women**—"All the women went after Miriam. . . . Sing ye unto the Lord" (Ex. 15:20–21).

  II. **Political Women**—"All the women that were wise-hearted did spin" (Ex. 35:25).

 III. **Listening Women**—"Joshua read the law before the women" (Josh. 8:35).

 IV. **Honorable Women**—The elite of the Lord's own are the true nobility (Ps. 45:9).

  V. **Beholding Women**—Among those who viewed the sufferings of Christ were those who were said to be "Beholding afar off" (Matt. 27:55).

VI. **Praying Women**—Of the disciples who were endued with power at Pentecost, it is said, "They continued in prayer with the women" (Acts 1:14).

VII. **Holy Women**—They are worthy of imitation (1 Peter 3:5).

F. E. Marsh

THE VIRTUOUS WOMAN

Proverbs 31:10–31

All of us have had or now have mothers. The writer of Proverbs was a competent judge of what it meant to be a "virtuous woman." This is his testimony:

I. **A wife. "The heart of her husband doth safely trust in her."**

A. Basis of true affection is perfect confidence; when this is shattered true happiness is gone.

B. Some men go wrong in spite of wives: for example, Pilate. Bible teaches many go wrong *because* of wives: e.g., Adam, Solomon, Haman. Only one did right in spite of evil, Job, but he was almost perfect.

C. The power and influence of a good wife:

The woman's cause is man's; they rise or sink
Together, dwarfed or godlike, bond or free;
If she be small, slight natured, miserable,
    How shall men grow?

D. Ruskin in *Queens' Gardens* says Shakespeare has no heroes, only heroines.

II. **A mother. "Her children rise up and call her blessed."**

A. Industrious, not ashamed of honest toil; Jesus dignified labor.

B. Domestic, not impatient in narrow sphere of home.

C. Self-controlled, "in her tongue is law of kindness."

D. "A woman that feareth the Lord."

S. R. D.

MOTHERHOOD AT ITS BEST

Proverbs 31:31

Qualities of true motherhood:

1. Care (in the form of love and service).

2. Comradeship.

3. Counsel.

4. Communion with God.

5. Comfort (Isa. 66:13).

6. Constancy (John 19:25).

Snappy Sermon Starters

A MOTHER'S CODE

Proverbs 1:8

What is the law of motherhood that our text admonishes us to follow?

1. A glorious commitment is the commitment of motherhood in bringing new life into the world. The knowledge of her responsibility drives the mother to God.

2. The next outstanding feature of the law of motherhood is its magnificent purpose. It brings a shapeless life into form, guiding, nurturing and loving it until its birth and after.

3. A mother's code also includes the liberal surrender of rights—as do all properly balanced codes.

4. Another feature of a mother's code is the thing that underlies all the codes of civilized nations today—confidence in people.

5. One more feature of a mother's code is its frequent addition of amendments.

Joseph B. Baker

BUILDING VESSELS FOR ROUGH SEAS

Proverbs 22:6

Introduction:

    A. Like the keels of ships, there are fundamental elements in the formation of character which will give greater safety in rough seas.

    B. Who are the builders of character?

        1. Day school teachers.

        2. Sunday school teachers.

        3. Parents.

    C. Note what is involved in the building of character:

  I. That Which Restrains or Makes Demands.

    A. Obedience—to law and authority.

    B. Reverence—for God and rights of others.

  II. That Which Releases or Helps to Expand.

    A. Wise observation of individual differences.

    B. Skillful guidance of individual potentialities.

    C. Watchful protection of individual tendencies.

  III. That Which Relates Life to God's Commands.

    A. Character must be imbued with just principles.

    B. Character must be motivated by goodly example.

Conclusion:

Romans kept example before children by placing busts of revered ancestors in their homes.

E. S. Phillips

THE INFLUENCE OF MOTHERS

Psalms 142:4

Introduction:

Souls may be saved in the home by the right use of the facilities there.

  I. The worth of a soul.

    A. The soul will continue to exist forever.

B. The righteous person will spend eternity happily, and the unsaved in misery.

C. The value of the soul is proved by the price Christ paid for it, His own life.

II. Contrast the care man takes for his soul and the soul of his fellow men, and the care he takes for worldly objects.

A. Is solicitude manifested for riches?

B. Are the children "properly" educated?

C. Are dress, honor, business, etc., overemphasized?

D. Is there anxiety in life?

E. Our care for souls and our concern for Christ's care do not come up to these manifestations.

III. Some facts that show care does not exist.

A. Secret prayer is missing.

B. Soul burden is missing.

C. Family prayer is neglected.

D. There is neglect of the prayer meeting.

Conclusion:

It is the responsibility of the mother to fulfill her task.

FIVE DEVOUT MOTHERS

I. Sarah (Gen. 21:6).

II. Hannah (1 Sam. 1:22).

III. Elisabeth (Luke 1:41).

IV. Mary (Luke 1:46).

V. Eunice (2 Tim. 1:5).

Snappy Sermon Starters

THE CORONATION OF MOTHERHOOD

And the king rose up to meet her and bowed himself . . . and caused a seat to be set for the king's mother; and she sat on his right hand (1 Kings 2:19).

This little incident in the routine of a busy king's court is a reminder of the age-long veneration of mothers. In this circumstance, it seems to have taken the form of an unofficial coronation. In our own calendar of the twentieth century the extended observance has emphasized farther this analogy.

1. It was recognition of authority manifested in sympathetic interest. This new form of sovereignty, growing out of Christianity, is echoed by Kipling in his familiar, "If I were hanged on the highest hill, Mother o' Mine, I know whose love would follow me still."

2. Authority asserted through years of comradeship. Hence Theodore Roosevelt could say, "Mothers are our foremost citizens." Busy mothers of today, occupied too often with social diversions, may forget this responsibility.

3. Authority of personal influence and example. Recall mothers of Wesley, Ruskin, Phillips Brooks, Frances Willard, and Harriet Beecher Stowe.

4. Authority delegated from God the Father. Surely Mary the Virgin mother, who was called of God for her special mission, is evidence of this fact, which history and religion have verified throughout all time.

Selected

AN APPOINTMENT WITH THE LORD

1 Samuel 1:20–28; 2:1–11

I. **A Christian mother's most important daily activity is prayer.**
   A. Her secret of success as a mother lies in spending time alone with the Lord each day.

B. Many feel that the best time for meeting the Lord is in the early morning hours.

C. Prayer should not be a monologue but a dialogue, with the Lord speaking through His written Word as His child speaks to Him.

D. The Bible is full of references to early morning prayer.
1. Abraham prayed in the morning (Gen. 19:27).
2. Moses prayed in the morning (Ex. 24:4).
3. Joshua prayed in the morning (Josh. 6:15).
4. Hannah and Elkanah prayed in the morning (1 Sam. 1:19).
5. Job prayed in the morning (Job 1:5).
6. David prayed in the morning (Ps. 63:1).

II. **Make an appointment with the Lord for early tomorrow morning and every morning after that.**

III. **Let God have His way in your life to make you the mother you should be.**

Selected

THE SPIRITUAL BEAUTY OF MOTHERHOOD

Psalm 90:17

Introduction:

The beauty referred to in this verse is not the beauty of God in Himself, but the beauty of God in and upon His children. We would like to think of this beauty as it relates to motherhood.

I. **This Beauty Is Varied.**
A. There is the beauty of *faith* as seen in Abraham and Sarah.
B. There is the beauty of *patience* as seen in Job.
C. There is the beauty of *purity* as seen in Joseph.
D. There is the beauty of *meekness* as seen in Moses.
E. There is the beauty of *thankfulness* as seen in David.
F. There is the beauty of *faithfulness* as seen in Daniel.
G. There is the beauty of *love* as seen in John.

II. **This Beauty Is Growing.**
It resembles the progress of light.
A. First comes the twilight.

B. Then comes the dawn.

C. Then comes the noonday.

III. This Beauty Is Unfading.

Mere physical beauty grows until it reaches full bloom and then begins to fade.

A. Not so with the beauty of God as seen in mothers.

B. It grows brighter and brighter through the years.

C. This beauty defies all the ravages of time, care, disease.

IV. This Beauty Attracts.

A. It draws the eyes of the unsaved.

B. It causes wonder.

V. This Beauty Is Unconscious.

A. A mother gives of herself unstintingly to the extent that she may lose her health.

B. Yet the beauty that shines through because of her devotion to others is wonderful.

C. She is too absorbed in her devotion to be aware of her beauty.

VI. This Beauty Is Rare.

A. It is rare and yet free, rare and yet attainable.

B. What a wonder that this beauty should be so uncommon yet so free.

adapted from *John Dunlop*

MOTHER—GOD'S MERCHANT SHIP

Proverbs 31:14

I. Mothers and ships are both products of a world other than the world in which they operate.

A. The ship is a land product operating in water.

B. A mother is a heavenly product operating on earth.

II. Merchant ships and mothers are also alike in that they are both bearers of wealth.

III. Mothers and merchant ships are alike in their relation to the magnetic center of the universe.

IV. Mothers and merchant ships are both harbingers of a new era.

A. Merchant ships with their missionaries, sewing machines, books, food, etc., have lifted backward peoples out of their isolation and put them in touch with the world.

B. Mothers are behind the great men of the world and are often the spiritual forces behind the scenes.

V. Mothers and merchant ships are alike in their speed. Mothers speedily care for their loved ones and anticipate their needs.

VI. Mothers and merchant ships are alike in that they both conceal their wealth.

VII. A mother is like the merchant ship in that neither take much rest.

VIII. If your mother is like a merchant ship, she is worthy of all your care.

A. If she still lives, visit her often.

B. If she is gone, allow the thought of her to color all your activity.

C. Honor your mother by living as she would have you live.

Joseph B. Baker

THE DIVINE MOTHERHOOD

Isaiah 66:13

Introduction:

Here is used one of the highest of human relationships to reveal God. We use other earthly relationships to describe God's love and care for us, but the thought of motherhood is perhaps most adaptable—and should certainly not be omitted. We must keep in mind, however, that God's love transcends even the love of motherhood. God's love is marked by:

I. Closest Intimacy.

A. The child's life, at its beginning especially, is a part of its mother's life.

B. The child is supported by maternal sustenance.

C. The child is watched over by maternal wisdom.

D. The child is wrapped up in maternal love.

E. Even more intimate is our relationship to God, for "we are His offspring."

II. Intense Individualism.

A. The mother individualizes her children.

B. God individualizes us in His dealings with us.

III. Unwearying Care.

A. The devotion of a mother is not that of hours or days, but a full-time devotion.

B. A mother's love and devotion are not exhausted when the object of that love leaves the home.

C. A mother never forgets her child.

D. Even more faithful is God's love for His children.

IV. The Sacrifice of Love.

A. All true love is sacrificial.

B. A mother's love is especially this.

Conclusion:

Motherhood means a life of sacrificial, often unhonored and un-requited, love, but what if that love is revealing God?

adapted from *U. R. Thomas*

JOCHEBED

Hebrews 11:23; Exodus 2:1-10; 6:20

I. Jochebed, the mother of Moses, is included among the "great cloud of witnesses" given in Hebrews chapter eleven. She is another of the Old Testament's models of motherhood.

A. Jochebed was a Levite by birth.

B. She gave birth to Moses, as we know, during the period when Pharaoh had commanded the Hebrews to throw all male born children into the Nile.

C. She had two other children—Miriam, probably twelve years old, and Aaron, three years old.

D. Picture, if you can, Jochebed's tense anticipation after she gave birth to Moses until she heard that he was a male child.

Since he was a male it meant that his life, and hers, were in danger. In spite of that, however, she provided for him at the risk of her own life.

II. Her maternal grief makes Jochebed a heroine.

A. She determined to fight for the life of her child in spite of the dangers.

B. The name Moses means "fair to God."

1. Jochebed undoubtedly realized that God had sent Moses for a purpose.

2. He was not really her own child, but one sent from God.

III. God's love and understanding for Jochebed are revealed in the fact that it was only a few short hours after Moses was placed in the Nile that Pharaoh's daughter saw him and took him as her own. Another indication of God's love is the fact that Jochebed was chosen to be Moses' nurse.

IV. Jochebed is an example or type of what all mothers suffer as far as anguish is concerned.

A. A man cannot appreciate the acuteness of the anguish a mother suffers. Even today, mothers are called upon to suffer in moments of travail in such a way that men cannot understand.

B. After the birth of children, mothers continue to suffer as they watch their children in the grasp of disease and pain.

C. Their courage is an example of the greatest courage and bravery.

D. Spiritually, too, mothers must suffer as they strive for the soul of their children.

E. Of such mothers it may still be said, "her faith hath saved her child."

adapted from *Abraham Kuyper*

SARAH

Hebrews 11:1–16

I. Sarah is the first woman whose faith is called to the attention of the Bible reader.

A. Her strength is particularly pointed out in her function as a married woman.
>   1. Paul points this out in Hebrews 11:11, where he acknowledges that by faith she became a mother.
>   2. Peter acknowledges the truth of this in 1 Peter 3:6.
B. Sarah is drawn true to life.
>   1. Her life as it is presented was actually experienced in those days of feminine self denial.
>   2. One thing distinguishes Sarah from others in her condition—the mystery of faith accomplished in her heart.

II. As a wife, Sarah fulfilled all the demands of God's precepts.

A. God had said that woman should be subservient to man.

B. Sarah sought her satisfaction in obeying her husband (going with him when he obeyed God's command, etc.).

C. She remained faithful to Abraham, even after being abducted to the harems of two strange princes.

D. She entertained his guests—angels unawares.

E. She gave him Hagar in preference to seeing him die childless.

III. Thus she regained the position of dignity which God had appointed for woman.

A. First Sarah rejected herself—coming to the belief that she was not to share Abraham's honor as the one from whom the Messiah was to arise.

B. She even hesitated to believe God's promise to her.

C. She finally did, however, come to believe and have faith.

IV. Because of this, God by His spirit strengthened and caused her faith to grow.

A. In that way she became the mother of Isaac and through him the mother of the Messiah.

B. Thus she is an example to all Christian women, in spite of her sinful moments—an example of living by faith.

adapted from *Abraham Kuyper*

THE MOTHER OF US ALL

1 Timothy 2:13–14

I. The name, Eve, means "mother of life" or "mother of all who have life." As a woman, and the first woman, Eve embodied potentially all that is female.

  A. In her lay concealed the kernel of a woman's grace and independence.

  B. Her susceptibility to Satan was also inherent in her.

  C. Her susceptibility to the faith was equally prominent in her.

II. Eve was created out of Adam.

  A. Adam, however, did not make her—she was created by God.

  B. God did not make Eve out of Adam, but took only one of the elements of human life from Adam from which to construct Eve.

III. Satan knew that the only way to reach Adam was to seduce Eve.

  A. He recognized her beauty.

  B. He also was aware of her natural frailty, and that she was the most temptable of the two.

   1. Woman represents human grace to a peculiar degree.
   2. Her sensibilities are more alert to the concrete and attractive.
   3. Eve's sin was essentially less profound than Adam's in that Adam must have realized what his transgression would bring about.
   4. Instead of lifting Eve up to be with himself, Adam fell with her and allowed himself to be drawn down.

IV. As a result of her fall, Eve had the good things God had given her taken away.

  A. Instead of the beauty of Paradise, she had to enter a world of thorns and thistles.

  B. Instead of a pain-free existence, she entered a world of pain, particularly as involves childbirth.

  C. Instead of a life of complete reliance upon God and the joy and assurance such a life gives, she entered upon a life of self-reliance and misery.

V. However, in spite of her failures, God in the soul of this woman sowed the seeds of a glorious faith.

A. Her seed was later to bruise the head of the tempter.

B. In her finite understanding, she assumed that Cain was the seed promised.

C. This seed was the child Jesus, born of Mary.

D. In this light, Eve is truly "mother of us all"—an encouragement to each one of us to realize that God does not cast us out simply because we err.

adapted from *Abraham Kuyper*

M-O-T-H-E-R

2 Timothy 1:5

Introduction:

A. Ours is a day of pronounced abbreviations: TV, NATO, UN, etc.

B. M-O-T-H-E-R is as old as the race, and it is significant that we have tried to spell out its meaning in verse, sermon and song.

I. **Is it not significant that mother is pronounced similarly in many different languages? Our efforts to spell out the meaning of mother are fully justified:**

M—mercy and meekness
O—others, the basic concept of motherhood
T—tenderness, tears, and truth
H—heart, hand, and helpfulness
E—endeavors, endurance, and enthusiasm
R—righteousness, reconciliation, and restoration

II. **"The hand that rocks the cradle is the hand that rules the world."**

A. If it is only the hand of a teenage baby-sitter, we will develop a juvenile society. If it is the hand of a riotous mother, we will develop a society of such caliber.

B. If it is the hand held out to God for guidance, then *mother* will continue to be a noble word—one with influence.

Fred Reedy

LOIS, THE GRANDMOTHER OF TIMOTHY

2 Timothy 1:5

    I. Lois is the one "grandmother" of the Scriptures.

        A. In her is revealed the peculiar significance of the grandmother in the family.

        B. She represents the Spiritual influence which can issue from her peculiar position.

        C. Lois was a believing woman.

            1. She was probably dead at the time Paul sent his second letter to Timothy, but he confirmed in that letter that she had lived in unfeigned faith.

            2. Paul relates that faith as revealed to Timothy as one of the links which brought Timothy to the Lord.

            3. Not only was Timothy descended physically from Lois, but also spiritually.

    II. While Lois was a believer, that did not automatically mean that her descendants would become believers. Through her faithful life, however, she was used of the Lord to lead her descendants to Him.

    III. Sometimes the direct descendants of a Christian mother do not find the Lord.

        A. In these cases, many times only those of a second or third generation find the Lord.

        B. Still, it remains the first duty of a Christian mother to live a faithful Christian life.

    IV. A grandmother can impart what the mother, because of her briefer experience and busier life, cannot give.

        A. Thus it is true that a grandmother has a peculiar and important ministry.

        B. She must give both mother (her daughter) and children (her grandchildren) that higher and unique blessing which an aged woman with a rich spiritual experience alone can give.

        C. Because of her peculiar influence, a grandmother should not set out to win the primary devotion of her grandchildren, excluding the mother.

D. The relationship of Lois, Eunice, and Timothy is an ideal one and should be the desired relationship of present-day generations.

adapted from *Abraham Kuyper*

THE SOUL-MOTHER

Romans 16:13

The mother of Rufus was a woman in the lowest stratum of society, for "Rufus" means "Red" and was a common name for Roman slaves. Somewhere along the way, however, she had "mothered" Paul, that poor pioneer of the Cross.

I. It is small wonder then, that Paul greets her in such terms. Soul-mothers are not necessarily those who provide homes for small children.
A. Think of those women who marry widowers with children.
B. Think of those who marry men with dependent parents.
C. To adore a child of your own flesh and blood is to love yourself and to dote upon an adopted child is to yield to the attraction of affinities, but to pour out a woman's heart in circumstances like the above is real love.
D. Think of those women who do missionary work among the heathen and in the slums.
E. Think of all those women who teach the children of others in public schools and Sunday schools.

II. Soul-mothers are not always women. Think of the men, rich and poor alike, who have devoted themselves to the welfare of others.
A. Abraham Lincoln.
B. The five missionaries to the Aucas.
C. Dr. Livingstone.

III. Think of all the wives who in some ways at least "mother" their husbands—not in an unhealthy way, but in the sense that they give comfort and strength and help, even businesswise.

Joseph B. Baker

EUNICE, THE MOTHER OF TIMOTHY

2 Timothy 1:5

I. Eunice was a channel of blessing. As such, she is a great model for motherhood.

A. She carried on in the same "unfeigned faith" of her mother Lois.

B. This same "unfeigned faith" was passed along to Timothy. This was not an automatic process, but a process of witnessing and example.

II. So great was the faith of Lois and Eunice, that Paul commends it.

A. Paul records her accomplishments as a mother to inspire a real and fervent faith in Timothy.

B. He characterizes her faith as consistent and constant.

C. He points out the importance of Christian training in the home.

III. Eunice is symbolic of Christian motherhood.

A. She carried out her responsibility as a Christian mother to witness and to teach Timothy.

B. She undoubtedly spent much time in prayer for her child.

IV. Fathers too have a blessed responsibility.

A. But a father can hardly be successful without the tender spiritual operation of a pious, faithful and praying mother.

B. It is the mother's responsibility to begin the spiritual training when the child is still young.

adapted from *Abraham Kuyper*

A GOOD MOTHER

Proverbs 19:14; 31

Introduction:

A man who has had a good mother is at a distinct advantage. A true mother:

I. Can Be Relied upon Always (31:10–12).

A. "Her price is far above rubies" (31:10).

B. "Her husband doth safely trust in her" (31:11).

II. **Has a Solution to Every Problem (31:13–16).**
   A. "Worketh willingly" (31:13).
   B. "Riseth also while it is yet night" (31:15).

III. **Is an Untiring Worker (31:17–22).**
   A. "Strengtheneth her arms" (31:17).
   B. "Her candle goeth not out by night" (31:18).
   C. "She is not afraid" (31:21).

IV. **Has a Spirit Which Draws Our Love (31:25).**
   A. "Strength and honor" (31:24).
   B. "In her tongue is the law of kindness" (31:26).

Conclusion:
   The rewards of a good mother (31:28–31).
   A. "Her children . . . call her blessed" (31:28).
   B. "Her own works praise her" (31:31).

Leslie Parrott

THE WIDOWED MOTHER

Luke 18:3

I. The finest courage in the world is demanded of those called upon to suffer widowhood. The widow mentioned by Jesus in our text is one of an innumerable multitude who would not give up.
   A. In the financial realm widows must prove themselves supreme in strategy.
   B. In the realms of domestic and cultural affairs, widowed mothers have reared some of history's greatest men and women.
      1. Washington was the son of a widow.
      2. Moody was fatherless from the age of five.

II. Widowed mothers have made glorious records outside the home. Many mothers have valiantly given their sons to war.

III. It is a sad fact that many mothers are not appreciated by their children. Real men have always been considerate of their mothers, especially of widowed mothers.

A. Washington wrote to his mother first when he received news that he had been elected President of the United States.

B. Garfield, before applauding thousands, embraced his widowed mother and expressed his appreciation for her.

Joseph B. Baker

A FATHER ENCOURAGES HIMSELF IN THE LORD HIS GOD

1 Samuel 30:6

We as families may encourage ourselves today as David did:

I. By reading and studying God's Word (Ps. 119:105; Rom. 10:17; Ps. 119:130).

II. By communicating with God in prayer (Acts 12:5; 4:18, 31; Matt. 7:7).

III. By seeking the fellowship of God's people (Acts 4:23; 1 Kings 19:9–19; Acts 14:21–22).

IV. By attending the seasons of Divine worship (Acts 2:42; Heb. 10:25; Acts 9:31).

V. By gathering about the Lord's Table (Acts 20:7; Josh. 4:6–7; 1 Cor. 11:23–30).

VI. By ministering to those who are in need (Acts 9:36, 39; 3:6; Gal. 6:1–9).

VII. By looking for the Coming of the Lord (Heb. 6:19; 10:37; Phil. 3:20–21).

Conclusion:
Truly, the family is the key in this business of living for the Lord.

C. C. Maple

WHAT GOD WILL DO FOR HIS CHILDREN

Ezekiel 34:11–30

As the unbelief of some cannot make the faith of God without effect (Rom. 3:3), neither can the unfaithfulness of God's shepherds make the faithfulness of God to fail. With regard to His children:

I. He will search out and seek them (v. 11).
They shall hear His voice (John 10:27).

II. He will deliver them (v. 12).
The power of the enemy shall not hold them.

III. He will bring them (v. 13).
Separate them for Himself.

IV. He will feed them (v. 14)
Bring them into good pastures (Ps. 23).

V. He will rest them (v. 15).
Cause them to lie down.

VI. He will bind up the broken (v. 16).
Broken and useless members.

VII. He will strengthen the weak (v. 16).
Weak through sickness and weariness.

VIII. He will judge their cause (vv. 17–22).
When tempted, annoyed and persecuted.

IX. He will watch over them (vv. 23–25; Heb. 13:20).

X. He will bless them and make them a blessing (v.26).

XI. He will abundantly satisfy them with good (vv. 29–31).

James Smith

FAITH OF OUR FATHERS FOR TODAY'S FATHERS

Hebrews 11

I. Abraham believed in the resurrection (Heb. 11:19).

II. Job believed it (Job 19:25–27).

III. David believed it (2 Sam. 12:22–23; Pss. 17:15; 49:15).

IV. Isaiah believed it (Isa. 26:19; 61:3).

V. Daniel believed it (Dan. 12:2).

VI. Paul believed it (Acts 17:21; 1 Thess. 4:16; 1 Cor. 15:52).

VII. Peter believed it (2 Peter 3:11–12).

VIII. The thief on the cross believed it (Luke 23:42)

A. B. Carrero

A FORTRESS FOR FATHERS

Thou therefore gird up thy loins, and arise, and speak . . . (Jer. 1:17–19).

I. Jeremiah commissioned as a witness. "Speak unto them all that I command thee." In this command is revealed a faith walk for fathers.

A. God's witness must be quick, ready. "Gird up thy loins." Today we would say: "Roll up your sleeves and get busy!" The first sign that a man is in earnest about any work is a gathering of his garments, so as to be unhampered and free.

B. God's witness must be bold, faithful. He must speak all that he is charged with. He must speak to all whom he is charged against. Why? Because he has no reason to fear man if he be faithful.

II. Why can he be so fearless? Because a sure stronghold is God. "I have made thee this day a defenced city." Enemy attacks shall be as against an "impregnable city," as against an unshakable "iron pillar," as against a "wall of brass."

III. "They will fight against thee." Expect opposition.

A. The vehemence of our foes.

B. The certainty of our security.

C. The source of our confidence. God's presence. God's promise. God's power.

Here is truly a faith for fathers in our modern day!

Selected

THE PARABLE OF THE TWO SONS

Matthew 21:28–31

Many of the Scribes and Pharisees exhibited the most deep-rooted and inveterate prejudice against the Savior's teaching and mission. Often they endeavored to catch Him in His sayings, that they might have some charge against Him. Jesus often therefore self-convicted

---

33

them, and out of their own mouths overwhelmed them with confusion. We have a striking instance of this in the passage connected with this subject. To show their perverseness, the Savior addressed to them this parable on fatherhood, and by their own confessions, He involved them in self-condemnation (vv. 31–32). Observe,

I. The Reasonable Commands of the Father. "A certain man had two sons, and he came to the first, and said, Son, go work today in my vineyard" (v. 28). Observe,

A. *The Nature of the Command.* "To work in the vineyard." Man was intended for labor.

B. *The Sphere of Labor Appointed.* The father's vineyard. A place in which the sons were personally interested. God's vineyard is His church.

C. *The Manner in Which the Command Was Delivered.* And said, "Son, go work today," etc. Here was nothing harsh or tyrannical. He speaks with authority, but it is the authority of a parent.

D. *The Period of Labor Required.* "Go work today." Daytime is working time. There is light for working, and opportunity also.

II. The Strange and Diversified Answers of the Sons.

A. The first said, "I will not." What disobedience, insolence, and rebellion. A direct and impertinent refusal. Surely of this abandoned son there could be no hope.

B. The second said, "I go, sir." Here was respect, submission, and promised obedience. How forcibly and beautifully it contrasts with the rebellious rudeness of the other. God demands the reverence and fear of His creatures. Divine things and claims must be treated with seriousness and respect. But observe,

III. The Conduct of the Sons Which So Strangely Contrasted with the Answers Given.

A. *The Rebellious Son Becomes Penitent and Obedient.* Such were the publicans and sinners to whom John the Baptist preached. So also the publicans and sinners to whom the Savior preached.

B. *The Courteous Son Turns Out to Be Disobedient and Deceiving.* All he did was to be civil and promise fairly. For of him it is said, "He went not." Such were the Scribes and Pharisees. They believed not in Christ. They were not sincere workers of godliness before the Lord. How fearfully this will apply:

1. To many children of religious parents. They attend

with them on the means of grace. They are moral, respectful in their religious conversation, they promise fair, but "go not."
2. To many who regularly frequent the House of God. They attend, and listen, and seem interested; but they do not move out in repentance and holiness.
3. It is a faithful picture of many professors. All their religion is in name, in show—in outside appearance. They do not walk in Christ's vineyard. They are not spiritual—or useful—trees; they bear leaves without fruit. Cyphers, cumberers of the ground. How terrible this state! How awful their doom!

Learn that

1. The grace of God can save the vilest of sinners.
2. Experimental and practical religion is "to love God, and to love others."

adapted from *Jabez Burns*

THE NURTURE AND ADMONITION OF THE LORD

Ephesians 6:4

There is no duty the claims of which will be more readily acknowledged, or the neglect of which will expose a man to more severe and merited condemnation, than that of the parent to the child. It needs no argument to establish it, for it is the natural outgrowth of one of the purest and deepest instincts of the heart. No right-minded man needs to be convinced of his obligations to his child, for he welcomes them, and instead of feeling them to be a burden, finds in their discharge one of his sweetest pleasures.

I. The Nature and Extent of Parental Influence.

It is evident that there is no relation in which a man exerts so much power for good or evil.

II. The Spirit and Manner in Which This Responsibility Should Be Discharged.

To make the unconscious influence which a man exerts a blessing, the one thing which is necessary is high-toned Christian principle. The power which goes forth from a man will be according to the Spirit that is in him, will be out of harmony with the tone of his life and character, but by his consistent daily work; and especially will this be the case with those of his own household.

A. Words may have power, but it is by deeds that abiding influence is to be gained.

Speech is silvery, but the silent eloquence of a holy life is golden, and the impression which it will produce is impossible to exaggerate. Christian parents, you love your children, you desire that they should serve and love Him whom you rejoice to call Master and Lord. Let them feel the depth and fullness and intensity of your love to Him. Let them see how it colors all your thoughts, sanctifies all your feelings, molds all your life. Let them, in a word, feel that your religion is your life. So may you not only save your own souls, but those over which God has made you overseers.

B. Looking now at the direct work of training, the first essential to a successful training is that you should set clearly before your own mind the object which you have in view.

You have to educate your child and educate him from the earliest years. Of course, such education by a Christian man must be religious. To train his children in the "nurture and admonition of the Lord," he feels to be at once a duty and a joy.

He who would really give such education must make it his business, to which everything else must, if necessary, be sacrificed, to train his children to be God-fearing men. "Seek ye first the kingdom of God and His righteousness," must be his motto in this as in every other department of life.

Fathers, if we desire to see our children Christians, we must teach them by word and deed, by precept and example, the old lesson of Solomon, "Wisdom is the principal thing; therefore get wisdom, and with all thy getting, get understanding."

Adapted from *Outlines of Sermons for Special Occasions*

THE DUTY OF FATHERS TO THEIR CHILDREN

They should:

I. Love them (Titus 2:4).

II. Train them up for God (Prov. 22:6; Eph. 6:4).

III. Instruct them in God's Word (Deut. 4:9; 11:19; Isa. 38:19).

IV. Rule them (1 Tim. 3:4, 12).

V. Correct them (Prov. 13:24; 19:18; 23:13; 29:17; Heb. 12:7).

GOOD FATHERS

Good fathers should:

I. Pity their children (Ps. 103:13).

II. Provide for their children (2 Cor. 12:4; 1 Tim. 5:8).

III. Pray for their children (1 Chron. 29:19; Job 1:5; John 4:46–49).

"OUR FATHER WHICH ART IN HEAVEN"

I. The Father's love
   A. In its nature
   B. In its degree
   C. In its comparison
   D. In its duration

II. The Father's prerogative

III. The child's obligation

FAMILY RELIGION

Joshua 24:15

A more striking scene can scarcely be beheld than that exhibited in this history. Joshua, the servant of the Lord and the successor of Moses, at the head of a large household, with a countenance which godliness and age had made serene and venerable, publicly announcing his own personal regard to religion, and offering his example to be followed of all the tribes of Israel. The assembly was large and they felt their obligations to him. The manner of his address is at once authoritative and persuasive.

I. The import of this resolution, in regard to the master of a family himself.

II. The influence of this resolution in his conduct toward those under his care.

III. The family constitution is intended for the good of humanity—religion will advance temporal interests of family. It will promote domestic happiness.

A. It is the duty of heads of houses to look well after the morals of their families.

B. Carefully to instruct them in the principles of religion.

C. To maintain family worship regularly.

D. Obliging them to attend public worship.

E. To set before them holy example.

One reason why there is so little family religion in the world is the neglect of masters of families. How great is the condescension and goodness of the ever blessed God in deigning to dwell under our humble roofs. If our earthly dwellings are by His presence rendered so light, secure and happy, how glorious the home above.

S. Stennett

FAMILY FOUNDATIONS

Deuteronomy 33:27

Moses' farewell message to Israel might be summed up in these words: "Do not forget God, hold on to your faith, remember the law and the testimony, have no fear, go forward." And in the heart of this valedictory we find our text: "The eternal God is your refuge, and underneath are the everlasting arms." These foundations also apply in family living:

I. Some Modern Foundations.

A. MATERIALISM. We have been so busy with the superstructure—stocks, bonds, securities, investments, economics—that we have forgotten or minimized the importance of the foundation.

B. SKEPTICISM.

C. PAGANISM. Millions are now bowing to the gods of the nations.

II. What's Underneath the Child of God?

A. "ARMS." A person. Back of this universe is a personal Creator (Gen. 1:1; Ps. 19:1).

B. "ARMS." Love, support, refuge, redemption, for the individual: John 3:16; for the world: John 3:17.

C. "ARMS." Guidance, direction, over-ruling Providence.

Application: What's underneath?

1. Is it materialism, skepticism, paganism?
2. Or "the everlasting arms?"

J. H. Ness

THE HOME BEAUTIFUL

The ark of the Lord continued in the house of Obededom . . . blessed
(2 Sam. 6:11).

There have been magazines published on the theme, "The House Beautiful," but here is a secret for the home beautiful. The ark was not an ikon or fetish. It was a symbol of nearness to God.

1. Every home, rich or poor, humble or elaborate, may have this glory. Records show that homes recognizing this

"nearness" by prayer and teaching have pleasant associations and delightful memories.

2. Beauty of home life, after all, is in the character of the inmates. This beauty comes not from tapestries or paintings, but from parental influences through life and example.

3. It is a heritage easily bequeathed to children, thence to be carried to other homes. Such beauty makes very simple furniture attractive and glorifies the cottage as well as the mansion. There is an atmosphere which signifies the divine nearness. Reports show a decline in the conventional "family altar" because of changed conditions in the home. But there is still opportunity for creating this atmosphere of "nearness" through table grace, good literature, and personal loyalty to God. The atmosphere of religion can be sustained even today.

Selected

WHEN RESPONSIBILITY BECOMES A PRIVILEGE
WITH A BRIGHT PROMISE

Exodus 2:9

I. A Divinely Imposed Responsibility on Every Parent.

A. To receive the child as a gift from God. "Take this child" (see Ps. 127:3).

B. To "bring them up in the nurture and admonition of the Lord" (Eph. 6:4). These two words mean teaching, disciplining, and chastening.

II. What This Imposed Responsibility Implies.

A. Increase in stature—the physical. This is the development of a strong, healthy body.

B. Increase in wisdom—the mental. This is the development of mind, or a well-balanced education.

C. Increase in favor with God and man—the moral and spiritual. This is the indispensable preparation of soul.

III. What Are the Parents' Qualifications to Be, if They Would Assume Responsibility?

A. An experience of the transforming power of the saving grace of Jesus Christ in their own lives. They utterly fail if this be wanting.

B. A knowledge of God and His Word. Almost a casual reading of the fourth chapter of 1 John will convince anyone that such knowledge is necessary.

C. A deep concern, or passion, for the complete and full salvation of the child whom they have taken to nurture and admonish. For a picture of parental concern turn to Matthew 15:21–28. See and read carefully 2 John 4.

D. To have an experimental knowledge of power with God in prayer. Have a daring faith in the promises of God that refuses to be denied. Jesus in His ministry never denied such faith.

E. To keep constantly filled with the Holy Spirit (see Eph. 5:18). This admonition immediately precedes the instruction relative to the ideal family life.

F. Be a faithful member in a spiritual, soul-winning, New Testament church. The cooperation of fellow members is a great help. (See Gal. 6:1–2; Heb. 10:24–25).

IV. The Assurance of Eternal Reward for Work Well Done.

A. "I will give thee thy wages." "God is not unrighteous to forget your work and labor of love . . ." (Heb. 6:10). Read carefully Matthew 8:11; 1 Corinthians 3; 1 Thessalonians 2:19–20; Revelation 22:12.

John A. Ross

THE DUTY OF REVERENCE TO MOTHERS

Ye shall fear every man his mother (Lev. 19:3).

The command is remarkable in being contrary to most passages in Scripture where the father is put first. Here mother is put first. "Ye shall fear every man his mother and his father." Then again the word "fear" in this case is not quite synonymous with "honor" in the fifth commandment. It has rather more intensity of meaning, including the idea of reverence. God intended to put both parents on the same level. Both are to be feared, or reverenced, alike.

"Ye shall fear [reverence] every man his mother." God is speaking.

1. It is His command with blessing. "Children, obey your parents in the Lord, for this is right. Honor thy father and mother; which is the first commandment with promise..." (Eph. 6:1–3).

2. No exceptions allowed: "Every man."

3. It places a personal responsibility to reverence parents. It is a duty to God.

4. It is an evidence of being righteous (Lev. 19:2). Example: Jesus on the cross remembered his mother.

5. Reverence to parents shows reverence for God.

Selected

RELIGION AT HOME

And it was noised that he was in the house (Mark 2:1).

Take Christ home with you. That is what Zacchaeus did. Jesus said, "This day is salvation come to this house."

I.   Christ in the house cannot remain a secret. "It was noised that he was in the house." If Christ is in our hearts and homes it will soon be known that he is there.
     A. And he will become an attraction. "Many were gathered." "Unto him shall the gathering of the people be."
     B. He will become an instructor. "He preached the word unto them."
     C. He will become an inspiration to extraordinary effort. "They uncovered the roof."

II. Christ in the house is a great blessing to those outside. He not only blesses them with Divine instruction, but also with:
     A. The blessing of healing. "One sick of the palsy."
     B. The blessing of pardon. "Thy sins be forgiven thee."

III. Christ wants to dwell in our homes. "Behold, I stand at the door and knock." He will bring purity, joy and gladness with him. He sups with us. He becomes one with us. He becomes not alone a guest but a gracious host.

IV. Christ's cause has everything to hope for from Christian homes. The world is but a collection of homes. If Christ can but obtain entrance into each home, the world is won! Work for the home is strategic.

Selected

THE LOVE OF HOME

2 Kings 4:13

Introduction:

The woman of Shunem answers Elisha's question with touching simplicity evidencing a mind unsophisticated by the world and without ambition or respect to the world's honors and distinctions. The love of family and the love of home and country is essential to the best interests both of a country and of the church of Jesus Christ. This appears when we consider the following factors:

I. The situation of the family is unique in the early development and perfection of a healthy young life!

II. The home is the best school for early mental training. The most important training for the mind is received before the child goes into a school or situation in which he begins to receive formal education.

III. Family discipline regulates and restrains human passions.
    A. The family head is the father and in the ideal family situation the father is the disciplinarian.
    B. The mother, however, is usually the more active of the two in the actual conduct of the family situation.

IV. The home is influential in establishing good working habits—it is the birthplace of a sound and solid work ethic.

V. The love of home, kindred, and country calls for some of the highest and noblest qualities of human nature.

VI. The home is the most ideal soil for sowing the Gospel seed.

A. Love of home is not Christianity.

B. Patriotism is not Christianity.

C. Good character is not Christianity.

D. Christianity is Christ—and must be lived in the home as well as outside the home.

adapted from *Amos Blanchard*

HOW THE CHRISTIAN FAMILY LIVES THE LIFE

Colossians 3:1–2

I. Keep your heart (Prov. 4:23; James 1:27).

II. Keep your soul (Luke 9:25; Matt. 16:26).

III. Keep instruction (Prov. 4:13; Matt. 11:29).

IV. Keep the Word of God (Luke 11:28).

V. Keep yourself pure (1 Tim. 5:22; 1 Cor. 6:16–20).

VI. Do all things in His name (Col. 3:16–17).

VII. Do all things to His glory (1 Cor. 10:31).

A. B. Carrero

THE WORD OF GOD FOR THE FAMILY'S EVERY NEED

Philippians 4:19

I. It Furnishes the Foundation for Our Faith (Rom. 10:17).

Faith must have a basis on which to rest (John 20:31; Acts 8:12).

II. It Reveals to Man the Way of Salvation (Rom. 1:16).

The Bible is the story of human redemption (Rom. 5:12, 20–21).

III. It Is the Source of Spiritual Light (Ps. 119:130).

Where it is preached—light follows (Dan. 9:2; John 5:39).

IV. It Is the Source of Spiritual Life (1 Peter 1:23).

Born of the Spirit—where there is birth—life (Heb. 4:12; Ps. 19:7).

V. It Is the Source of Spiritual Food (Matt. 4:4).

Folk know where to go for natural food (1 Peter 2:2; Acts 11:21–24).

VI. It Will Build Believers Up in Righteousness (Acts 20:32).

Some folk never build up—wrong food (1 Cor. 11:30; Jude 1:20).

VII. It Will Be the Standard by Which We Are Judged (John 12:47–48).

Evidences in the Gospels, historical record in Acts, rule for Christian living in epistles (John 20:31; Rom. 5:17; 2 Peter 1:5).

C. C. Maple

HEAVEN LIKENED TO A FAMILY

Ephesians 3:15

The Christian is a traveler on his way to Zion. The Christian is a tempest-tossed sailor, sailing to the celestial haven, and often does he long to behold the quiet shores of the heavenly world. The Christian is a child of God, and an heir of glory, and he looks forward when he shall receive from the hands of the Chief Shepherd the crown of life, etc. Our subject leads us to the contemplation of the heavenly family. Now let us notice,

I. The Members of the Heavenly Family.

A. There is the supreme head of the family, God.

B. There is the elder brother, Jesus, the mediator between God and man.

C. There is an innumerable company of angels.

D. There will be a countless number of glorified children.

E. There will be the whole collected body of believers.

II. The Unity of the Heavenly Family.

The "whole family." Observe,

A. There is one family house—impossible on earth because of dissension.

B. All of this family have the same employments—worship.

C. All have the same enjoyments—fellowship with God.

III. The Glorious Characteristics of the Heavenly Family.

A. Absolute purity.

B. Perfect blessedness.

C. Glorious permanency.

Application:

1. Have we not all some friends and family who form part of the family in heaven?

2. Are we living and acting so as to get there ourselves?

3. Invite sinners.

adapted from *Jabez Burns*

THE PARENTAL CHARACTER OF GOD

Deuteronomy 32:6

The text is part of that celebrated and truly interesting song of Moses in which the wonderful acts of God's goodness to the children of Israel are celebrated. It also contains a sad record of the defections of Israel toward God. The text is a pointed interrogation respecting the return they had made to God for His goodness: "Do you thus repay the Lord, O foolish people, and unwise? Is he not your Father?"

Let us contemplate, God as the Father of His people, and the claims which He has upon His children.

Notice,

I. God as the Father of His People.

God is especially the Father of believers. Unconverted sinners are alienated from God. His image they do not bear; in His family they do not dwell; His authority they do not acknowledge.

A. God is the Author of their spiritual existence (1 Peter 1:3).

B. He makes paternal provision for His children.

C. He affords paternal protection to His children.

D. He imparts paternal instruction.

E. He takes paternal delight in His children (Isa. 66:13).

F. He administers paternal correction to His children (Jer. 30:11; Heb. 12:6).

As a Father,

G. He lays up a paternal provision for His children.

Notice,

II. The Claims Which He Has upon His Children.

A. He ought to receive from us the highest reverence.

B. He ought to have our Supreme affections.

C. He should possess our unwavering confidence.

D. He should have our cheerful obedience.

E. He should receive from us our most exalted praises.

adapted from *Jabez Burns*

FAMILY WORSHIP

Genesis 18:19

Let us consider the subject of family worship.

I. In the Basis of It.

A. Is it not grounded on the laws of our nature? God has stamped upon human nature the principle of parental regard and affection. Thus, parents feel pleasure in toiling to supply the wants of their offspring. He who neglects this does violence to his own nature, denies the faith, and is worse than an infidel. But are the minds, the precious souls of our children, of less value and importance than their bodies? Can it be supposed that the outer shell is to absorb our care, and that the jewel is to be neglected?

B. Have we not Scriptural precedents? (Job. 1:5; Josh. 24:15; 2 Sam. 6:20; Acts 10:2, etc.)

II. What Family Worship Should Comprise.

A. The reading of the Holy Scriptures (Deut. 6:6–7). Especially the Psalms, Proverbs, Ecclesiastes, and the Gospels, and the Epistles of the New Testament.

B. Songs of holy praise.

C. The offering up of prayer and supplication for ourselves, friends, church and the world.

Let us consider,

III. The Mode in Which It Should Be Conducted.
A. As to times and frequency.

Morning and evening if possible; at least, once a day.

B. Family worship times should be short and varied. Parents shouldn't tire or fatigue those younger members of the family who cannot be expected to feel much interest in it. Great wisdom and care are necessary, or the summons to the family altar will always throw a gloom over the buoyant, joyous, minds of children. Perhaps ten minutes ought never to be exceeded, except where there are no children.

C. All the members of the family, if possible, should be present.

D. It should be conducted with regularity and constancy.

IV. The Advantages Which We May Expect to Derive from It.
A. An increase of family knowledge.

B. The general possession of family harmony.

C. An exemption from family calamities, and the enjoyment of family blessedness.

V. Reply to Some Objections Made Against Family Worship.
A. For want of time.

This is a most thoughtless and unprincipled objection.

Not time to acknowledge God—to bless Him—to seek His favor? David and Daniel found time; so do Jews and Mohammedans.

B. For want of ability.

C. Not essential.

We refer to Jeremiah 10:25. It does appear essential to family order, safety, comfort.

Application:

1. Press this duty upon pious fathers and mothers.

2. Let young Christians prize it, and improve it. What is heaven, but one grand family where worship is ever celebrated? "They rest not day and night, saying, Holy,

holy, holy Lord God Almighty, which was, and is and is to come" (Rev. 4:8–11).

adapted from *Jabez Burns*

CHRISTIAN NURTURE OF CHILDREN

Proverbs 22:6

I. Faithful and patient nurture in godliness will abide.

II. Godly example and the teaching of wisdom by adults is a first duty.

III. Essential and eternal principles give spiritual poise through life.

IV. Children are teachable, precious souls, destined for eternity.

V. Children should be happy, helpful, hopeful, reverent, and generous hearted.

VI. Children should be gracious and thoughtful, and walk humbly with God.

VII. The way consists of love, courage, merciful justice, and help in trial.

VIII. The way consists of forgiveness, sacrifice, and knowledge divine.

IX. The way consists of deliverance from sin, goodness, purity, and peace.

X. May children grow as Christ grew, with the grace of God upon them.

Rev. Walter D. Mehrling

TRAIN THE CHILDREN

Proverbs 22:6

  I.   We train by example.

 II.   We train by precept.

III.   We train by efficient teaching of God's Word.

IV.   We train by carefully planned programs of worship and service.

O. T. Deever, DD.

THE CHRISTIAN FAMILY KEPT BY GOD'S POWER

1 Peter 1:5

   I.   Protected under the blood (Ex. 12:13).

  II.   Under the shadow of the Almighty (Ps. 91:1).

 III.   Hidden in His pavilion (Ps. 27:5).

  IV.   In secret communion (Ps. 31:20; Rev. 3:4).

   V.   In God's secret chambers (Isa 26:20; Ps. 17:8).

  VI.   Safe under His wings (Ruth 2:12).

 VII.   Covered by His armor (Eph. 6:13).

A. B. Carrero

IMPREGNABLE

The family is God's "safe" for preserving His children:

  I.   God Before (Isa. 52:12).

 II.   God Behind (Isa. 58:8).

III.   God Underneath (Deut. 33:27).

IV.   God Above (Song of Sol. 2:4).

 V.   God Round About (Ps. 125:2).

VI.   God in Them (1 John 3:24).

VII.   They in God (Col. 3:3).

VIII.   Preserved in Jesus Christ (Jude 1).

Twelve Baskets Full of Original Bible Outlines

FOUNDATIONS FOR A STRONG FAMILY

Therefore whosoever heareth these sayings of mine, and doeth them, I will liken him unto a wise man, which built his house upon a rock (Matt. 7:24–27).

I.   All men are building.

II.   All builders have a choice of foundations.

III.   All foundations will be tried.

IV.   Only one foundation will stand.

Selected

CHRISTIAN HOME ESSENTIALS

Exodus 2:1–4; Joshua 24:14–15; Ephesians 5:28–31; 6:1–4

I.   Mothers with a Godly background (Ex. 2:1).

II.   Mothers who properly value God-given children (Ex. 2:2).

III.   Mothers of God-pleasing character (Ex. 2:2–3).

IV.   Mothers who obey God before man (Ex. 2:2–3).

V.   Mothers who trust children to God's care (Ex. 2:2–3).

VI.   Mothers who act with God-given wisdom (Ex. 2:4).

VII.   Fathers who have courage of their convictions (Josh. 24:14–15).

VIII.   Fathers who give public testimony for God (Josh. 24:14–15).

IX.   Fathers who stand against sin (Josh. 24:14).

X.   Fathers who appeal for decision for God (Josh. 14:15).

XI.   Fathers who lead Godward (Josh. 24:14–15).

XII.   Fathers who rule their household for God (Josh. 24:15).

XIII.   Fathers who can stand for God courageously (Josh 24:15).

XIV.   Fathers who cannot be compromised (Josh. 24:15).

XV.   Fathers who serve God (Josh. 24:15).

XVI.   Fathers who appreciate God's blessing (Josh. 24:14–15).

XVII.   Husbands who love their wives (Eph. 5:28).

XVIII.   Husbands who provide for their wives (Eph. 5:29).

XIX.   Husbands who protect their wives (Eph. 5:29).

XX.   Husbands who properly estimate their wives (Eph. 5:30).

XXI.   Husbands who are inseparably linked with their wives (Eph. 5:31).

XXII.   Husbands who love their wives (Eph. 5:31).

XXIII.   Husbands who are loyal to their wives (Eph. 5:31).

XXIV.   Children who obey their parents (Eph. 6:1).

XXV.   Children who honor their parents (Eph. 6:2–3).

XXVI.   Children reared properly (Eph. 6:4).

Selected

CHRISTIAN LIGHT ON REARING CHILDREN

Deuteronomy 6:4–9, 20–25; 2 Timothy 3:14–15.

I. **The Homes Needed for Such Rearing (Deut. 6:4–9).**
   A. Homes where God is properly acknowledged.
   B. Homes where God is loved.
   C. Homes where God's Word is honored.
   D. Homes where God's Word is taught.
   E. Homes where God's Word is practiced.
   F. Homes where God's Word is publicly witnessed to—honored.

II. **The Parents Needed for Such Rearing (Deut. 6:20–25).**
   A. Parents who perpetuate God's truth.
   B. Parents who understand their Bible.
   C. Parents who can tell of God's wondrous work.
   D. Parents who believe in the value of obeying God.
   E. Parents who explain the value of obeying God.

adapted from *William McCarrell*

PLAY

Zechariah 8:5

Introduction:

Children play—that is one of the first things they do. Loving parents provide their children with the right kind of things to play with.

I. Play is a part of life.

A. A play room is as necessary as a living room.

1. If you do not provide a place for your children to play, they will be forced to find a place outside the home, a place where you cannot supervise their activities.

2. If you do not provide them with companions, they will go out and find their own.

3. If you do not give them time to play, they will steal it from time allotted for other things.

B. There is more to life, of course, than simply playing. There is a right time for play and a right time for other activities.

II. God likes to see children play.

A. An earthly father likes to see his children happy at play. Our heavenly Father too, likes to see children happy—and we are told time and time again to think of our heavenly Father in the framework in which we think of our earthly father.

B. Adults too need to play—although their activities will not be the play of children.

1. Play is a form of recreation, which is necessary to human existence.

2. Seek God's face in the matter of your leisure activities.

III. The laws of play are the laws of life. As a child learns to play, he also learns to work and to live.

A. One of God's laws is that a person should devote his entire self to work.

B. A person learns that as he learns to play he learns to work just as wholeheartedly.

C. One who cheats at play will also cheat in the game of life.

D. A child also learns many other lessons in living from play.

IV. **Parents must enjoy their children playing.**
Just as Zechariah in our text saw children playing even in the streets of Jerusalem where there was terrible suffering and bloodshed, so parents today must have a vision of their children playing in spite of developments which militate against this vision. It is a mother's duty and privilege to guide her children in the area of play and in the area of both physical and spiritual growth.

adapted from *Charles E. Jeffers*

CHILDREN—A HERITAGE OF THE LORD

Psalm 127:3

I. A gracious gift of God (Gen. 33:5).

II. A precious gift to Abraham (Josh. 24:3).

III. A sweet memory to Job (Job 29:4).

IV. A great happiness to parents (Ps. 127:4–5).

V. A wonderful blessing to Hannah (1 Sam. 1:27).

VI. A child under good training (2 Tim. 1:5; 3:15).

VII. Bring the children to the Lord (Matt. 19:14; Mark 10:14).

VIII. Bring them to the place of worship (2 Chron. 20:13).

A. B. Carrero

A WONDERFUL BABY

Exodus 2:2–11

A baby's birth is one of life's outstanding experiences. The birth of Moses was a great event. He was to be a deliverer of his people, a prophet of the Lord, and a type of Christ, our great Savior and King.

1. The baby BORN (v. 2). A great EVENT.

2. The baby HIDDEN (v. 3). A great SECRET.

3. The baby FOUND (v. 6). A great SURPRISE.

4. The baby NURSED (v. 9). A great PROVIDENCE.

5. The baby NAMED (v. 10). A great HOPE.

6. The baby GROWN (v. 11). A great BLESSING.

The special points in the wonderful birth and early experience of Moses illustrate the kind providence of God over every life that is dedicated to Him by prayer. In the life of Moses we see God's time, God's protection, God's providence, God's care, God's guidance, and God's blessing. The faith and prayer of Moses' parents secured all these things

C. E.

WHEN A CHILD BECOMES A MAN

When I was a child, I spake as a child . . . but when I became a man, I put away childish things (1 Cor. 13:11).

The law specifies a fixed age for the recognition of manhood. But we all know there is quite a variation. Some mature at eighteen; others at twenty-five. But the home is the proper place for maturation. Here is another standard:

I. **Sympathy with real issues of life.** Matter of broader thinking; maturing purpose.

II. **Appreciating love;** not the sentimental emotion, but the broad charity implied in Paul's message. One of the signs of manhood and womanhood—finer emotions.

III. **Taking God's plan into account.** "When Moses was come to years" (Heb. 11:24). Entering the Father's partnership. Prodigal son's new "resolve." "Servant." Instead of "give me"—"use me."

SINS AGAINST CHILDREN

Genesis 42:22

I. Depriving them of good parents.

II. Depriving them of the privilege of play.

III. Depriving them of good home life.

IV. Depriving them of value-centered secular education.

V. Failure to bring them up in the nurture and admonition of the Lord.

Selected

CHILDHOOD REVALUED

And he took a child, and set him in the midst of them (Mark 9:36).

This was an epoch-making event in the world's life. Nothing that Alexander the Great ever did had so much significance for human life as this act of Jesus. No one hitherto had ever done such a thing. He here honored what the world had cast aside as refuse. Child life has no meaning where the principles of the great Child Finder are not governing the ideals and conduct of the people. What did this act mean?

I. It meant **the recovery of a whole lost continent of human life.** He knew the wealth and undeveloped possibilities of this continent so long neglected by the world.

II. It meant **the recovery of lost principles of true living.** He desired to reveal certain qualities of soul and essential elements of character unrecognized by men of the day, but all of which qualified for His kingdom.

III. It meant **a revaluation of the elements of true greatness** in a world where men held warped and fantastic ideas of greatness. Caesar's sword, Pilate's power, Seneca's luxury were supposed to make these men great. The view of life found in the heart of the child is the open door to real greatness.

We are wise and faithful to our solemn trusts as parents and teachers if we know how effectively to do, with His purposes in our hearts, what Jesus did when "he took a little child." Woe betide the home, the church, the nation, if we fail to see the profound and moving significance of this beautiful act.

W. C. C.

CHRISTIAN HOME

But if a widow has children or grandchildren, they should learn first of all to put their religion into practice by caring for their own family and so repaying their parents and grandparents (1 Tim. 5:4 NIV).

Paul is giving counsel that seems obvious and elementary. But from his day to this his words have never ceased to be in point. While discussing the domestic problems of fatherless homes, he speaks a word concerning filial obligations that children of our day do well to cherish. He indicates that:

I.   Conduct at home is a prelude and promise of character that is to be.

II. A primary call of religion to youth is the meeting of duties in the home.

III. Parental sacrifices for children call for grateful recognition.

IV. Learning religion at home safeguards the spiritual destiny of children. Successful home life is a joint enterprise in which parents and children must lovingly cooperate. Recognition of God in the home through worship safeguards love, unity, and happiness in the household.
     A. There must be a visual form of recognition of God in the home. A simple ritual of worship objectifies the fact and place of God in daily life.

B. Domestic peace and genuine unity are guaranteed where households sincerely join in the worship of God.

C. Reverence and all other Christian virtues are best taught through organized worship in the household.

D. Worshiping households bless the world with a generation of Christian teachers—our only recourse for a strong, vital church. Let us unify and sanctify our home life by regular and joyous household worship.

Selected

LOVE AT HOME

And she had a sister called Mary, which also sat at Jesus' feet, and heard His word (Luke 10:39).

Martha sought to serve the Lord with her very best.

Mary was full of love to Jesus, as we know by her anointing Him, and therefore she also would serve Him with her very best.

She did so by attending to His words.

I. Love at Leisure. "Which also sat at Jesus' feet."
Like Mary—

A. We would feel ourselves quite at home with Jesus our Lord.

B. We would be free from worldly care—leaving all with Jesus. All our future, for time and for eternity, safe in His dear hands.

C. Let us, without fear, enjoy leisure with Jesus—leisure, but not laziness—leisure to love, to learn, to commune, to copy.

II. Love in Lowliness. "At Jesus' feet."

A. A penitent, which is an acknowledgment of my unworthiness.

B. A disciple, which is a confession of my ignorance.

C. A receiver, which is an admission of my emptiness.

III. Love Listening. "And heard His word."

A. Listening to Himself. Studying *Him*, reading His very heart.

B. Listening, and not obtruding our own self-formed thoughts, notions, reasonings, questionings, desires, and prejudices.

C. Listening, and forgetting the observations and unbeliefs of others.

God delights to deal with us when we are most in private: He appeared to Abraham sitting in the door of his tent (Gen. 18). The Holy Spirit came down upon the apostles, and filled all the house where they were sitting (Acts 2). The eunuch, sitting in his chariot, was called and converted by Philip's preaching (Acts 8).

—Henry Smith

Which shall we praise more, Mary's humility or her docility? I do not see her take a stool and sit by Him, or a chair and sit above Him; but, as desiring to show her heart was as low as her knees, she sits at His feet. She was lowly set and richly warmed with His heavenly beams. The greater submission, the more grace. If there be one hollow in the valley lower than other, that is where the waters go.

—Bishop Hall

Dr. Chalmers complained: "I am hustled out of my spirituality."

—Spurgeon

CHILDREN AND PARENTS

Leviticus 19:3; Ephesians 6:1–2

It seems eminently natural that the Bible, a Book which professes to be a guide for humanity, should have much to say concerning a relationship into which every living being enters. We do not all become husbands or wives or parents, but the very fact of existence implies that we are the children of some father and mother and that involves us in certain distinct and inviolable obligations. Even in the pitiful instances where death leaves children orphans, there are commonly those who assume the work of education and nurture; they stand *in loco parentis*, and therefore have the right to claim all the authority and to receive all the reverence which belong to the parental position. So it may fairly be said that the Scriptures speak to everyone, without exception, when they describe and exhort to filial duty. "Children, obey your parents in the Lord: for this is right. Honor thy father and mother." Let us, then, try to understand what obligations they involve, and inquire:

I. What Is Meant by Filial Obedience?

The great basal law of household life is that the will of the parent shall be supreme. Both father and mother are authorized to rule. This is according to direct Divine revelation and in entire harmony with nature. Children as they enter life are placed in the keeping of those who love them and who are responsible for them. God holds the parents responsible for the nourishment, right training, and holy development of their offspring. They are to mold the young mind and inspire the young heart. If parents fail to do this, they must give an account of their stewardship and receive the inevitable punishment. Shakespeare utters this same truth when he says:

> The voice of parents is the voice of gods,
> For to their children they are heaven's lieutenants;
> > To steer
> The wanton freight of youth through storms and
> > dangers
> Which with full sails they bear upon, and straighten
> The mortal line of life they bend so often.
> For these are we made fathers, and for these

May challenge duty on our children's part.
Obedience is the sacrifice of angels,
Whose form you carry.

Thus the authority of parents is grounded in the will of God, and it is their duty to insist upon obedience. They have no right to let the reins of government drop out of their hands for one moment.

II. What Is Meant by Filial Honor?

Many duties are included in this most comprehensive term, even that of obedience to parents. There are three ways especially in which sons and daughters honor their parents. *By reverence, care and confidence.* Their superiority in age and therefore in enlarged experience, demands that we should pay them due reverence. Children do not know everything, though sometimes in the flush of young attainments they speak and act as though they did. Reverence the counsel and judgment of parents, honor them for their motives and, where possible, agree with their methods.

As to the second element in this word honor—viz., *care of parents*—it ought to be necessary to say very little. But I find that Jesus Christ distinctly asserts that there is no higher religious duty than this. The first and most religious duty of human life is to care for the wants of parents who can no longer care for themselves. You do no higher service than when you give your strength and time and love to administer comfort to their need. This form of honoring parents, however, is sometimes sadly forgotten. Children are often selfish. The will draw all they can, and as long as they can, from their parents. Instead of offering help they seem to imagine that they have a right to be helped.

As to the third element of honor—*confidence*—I will only say that as far as in you lies let there be no barrier between you and your parents. Make them free of your secrets. Trust them absolutely. They deserve it of you and will repay it with a wealth of love and responsive confidence as you grow older of which you, perhaps, now have no conception. Obey and honor thus your father and mother, for it is right and it is the first commandment with promise.

adapted from *W. Braden*

TRAINING THE CHILD

Proverbs 22:6

This text is a vital message to parents. Hear it. We call attention to three things in the text:

I. The Reason for Training.
A. "Train up a child."
  1. The child is helpless.
  2. He is needy.
  3. He is wholly dependent.

B. Train the child because he is the heir of the past, the happiness of the present and the hope of the future.

C. Your child is your opportunity and responsibility from the Lord.

II. The Rule for Training.
"In the way he should go."

A. The training of the child should be upward.

B. The child should be led to salvation of the soul, to service of the life, and to safety for eternity.

III. The Results of Training.
A. "When he is old, he will not depart from it."
  1. The course of life is fixed in early days.
  2. The goal to be gained is given in youth.
  3. Abiding habits of life are fixed while children are young.

B. If the right course is fixed, if the ideal goal is given, and if righteous habits are formed in childhood, the same will be pursued in the years to come.

Sermons in Outline

AN OLD SERMON FOR YOUNG HEARERS

Remember now thy Creator in the days of thy youth (Eccl. 12:1).

We have here the primary obligation of human life, to remember the Creator. This should be intelligent, loving, practical, permanent, and it should begin in the choicest period of life, in "the days of our youth."

I. Whom Ought We to Remember?

A. Our Creator. We are indebted to Him for life itself, as also for health and strength and the powers of mind by which we are able to remember Him.

II. How Ought We to Remember Him?

A. To obey Him. To remember Him is to be obedient.

B. Remember Him to be thankful.

C. Remember Him to trust Him.

D. Remember Him to love Him, and therefore to serve Him.

III. Why Ought We to Do It in Our Youth?

A. Reverent obedience to God is the only method of having a life that shall be worth living.

B. Youth is the best time to begin. It is the time of susceptibility. For another reason, because it lengthens joy and Christian usefulness.

C. Because it is the easiest time to begin because of the comparative ease with which the duty may be performed.

D. Because the present is the only time we can command!

E. Because it is important to have the trend of life settled early in favor of the good.

F. Because cultivating the good life early will bless every subsequent period of being. It will result in more years given to Christ. Every year away from him is an empty year from the eternal point of view.

Selected